SPOTLIGHT ON AMERICAN HISTORY

George Washington
America's History Maker

Andrew Olesen

PowerKiDS press™

New York

Published in 2016 by The Rosen Publishing Group, Inc.
29 East 21st Street, New York, NY 10010

Photo Credits: Cover DEA Picture Library/Getty Images; p. 4, 7, 12, 18 Stock Montage/Archive Photos/Getty Images; p. 5 Lawrence Thornton/ Archive Photos/Getty Images; p. 8 Kean Collection/Archive Photos/Getty Images; p. 9 Print Collector/ Hulton Archive/Getty Images; pp. 11, 13, 15 Library of Congress Prints and Photographs Division; p. 17 GraphicaArtis/Archive Photos/Getty Images; p. 19 PhotoQuest/ Archive Photos/Getty Images; p. 20 Fotosearch//Archive Photos/Getty Images; p. 21 MPI/ Archive Photos/Getty Images

Library of Congress Cataloging-in-Publication Data

Olesen, Andrew.
George Washington : America's History Maker / Andrew Olesen. -- First edition.
pages cm. -- (Spotlight on American history)
Includes bibliographical references and index.
ISBN 978-1-4994-1754-8 (library bound) -- ISBN 978-1-4994-1751-7 (pbk.) -- ISBN 978-1-4994-1750-0 (6-pack)
1. Washington, George, 1732-1799--Juvenile literature. 2. Presidents--United States--Biography--Juvenile literature. 3. Generals--United States--Biography--Juvenile literature. 4. United States. Army--Biography--Juvenile literature. I. Title.
E312.66.O44 2016
973.4'1092--dc23
[B]

2015014336

Manufactured in the United States of America

CPSIA Compliance Information: Batch #WS15PK: For Further Information contact Rosen Publishing, New York, New York at 1-800-237-9932

CONTENTS

THE EARLY LIFE OF GEORGE WASHINGTON

George Washington is one of the most important people in U.S. history. He was the commander of the Continental army. He led the colonists to victory against the British during the American Revolution. In 1789, Washington was elected to be the first president of the United States.

This portrait of George Washington is an engraving created from a 1792 painting by John Trumbull. Washington is shown in the military uniform of the commander in chief of the Continental army.

This photograph, taken in 1955, shows Ferry Farm in Fredericksburg, Virginia. A ferry was used to cross the river between the farm and Fredericksburg.

George Washington was born to Augustine and Mary Ball Washington on February 22, 1732. He was born in the British colony of Virginia. George spent much of his youth learning about farming. He worked on the family farm, called Ferry Farm. The Washington family had moved to Ferry Farm when George was about six years old. George Washington learned how to plant and grow crops such as tobacco, fruits, vegetables, and grains. He also learned about the different tools that were needed to run a plantation.

As a young boy, George Washington's interests in math and exploring the nearby woods led him to study **surveying**. He practiced by mapping his half brother Lawrence's land.

Through Lawrence, George befriended the Fairfax family. Lawrence had married Anne Fairfax, who was related to Lord Fairfax. Lord Fairfax was a wealthy Englishman who controlled more than 5 million acres (2 million ha) of land in Virginia.

In 1748, Lord Fairfax decided to send a mapping party to explore his lands west of the Blue Ridge Mountains. George Washington was invited to join them. In July 1749, Lord Fairfax helped him get an important job. He became the official surveyor of Culpeper County, Virginia. He was paid well and saved his money. Soon he was able to buy his own land. By 1752, Washington had bought about 2,300 acres (930 ha) of land.

George Washington started his first job as a surveyor at the age of 17. This color print shows the young George Washington working as a surveyor in the mid-1700s.

THE FRENCH AND INDIAN WAR

In 1752, Washington became a major in the Virginia **militia**. In 1754, a war broke out between Britain and France over land in America. This was called the French and Indian War. On May 28, 1754, Washington and his men attacked a group of French soldiers. Ten French soldiers were killed, and 21 were taken prisoner. On July 3, 1754, the French struck back. They attacked Washington at Fort Necessity, and he was forced to give up.

This engraving shows General George Washington during the French and Indian War. He is seen reading prayers to the soldiers in his camp.

This engraving celebrates the recapture of Fort Duquesne from the French in November 1758 during the French and Indian War. George Washington's troops raise the British flag.

In 1755, Washington became an aide to Major General Edward Braddock. Braddock's goal was to drive the French out of Fort Duquesne. Instead, on July 9, 1755, the French and their Indian **allies** killed Braddock and many other soldiers. Washington barely escaped. After this battle, Washington was put in charge of Virginia's troops. He successfully drove the French out of Fort Duquesne. He then returned home and became a member of the Virginia **legislature**. In 1759, he married the widow Martha Dandridge Custis and settled into the life of a farmer.

COMMANDER IN CHIEF OF THE CONTINENTAL ARMY

After winning the French and Indian War in 1763, Britain had many **debts** to pay. It decided to tax the colonists to raise money to pay these debts. Many colonists would not pay the taxes. They felt the taxes were unfair. The colonists had no voice in Parliament. They had no one to represent their interests. This was known as taxation without representation.

After many protests by the colonists, including the Boston Tea Party, the American Revolution began. On April 19, 1775, the first shots of the Battles of Lexington and Concord were fired. This was the beginning of the American Revolution. On June 5, 1775, the Continental Congress named George Washington commander in chief of the Continental army.

The American Revolution did not begin well for America. The Continental army was outnumbered by the British soldiers. The British regulars also had better weapons and training. By the summer of 1776, Washington's forces had been driven from New York into New Jersey by the British. That winter, British troops entered New Jersey and forced Washington to run again, this time into Pennsylvania.

In this painting, Washington and his troops can be seen looking at the flags captured from the British troops during the Battle of Trenton.

Spirits were low among Washington's men. Washington knew he had to do something to show the British that the Americans could not be beaten so easily. He came up with a daring plan. He decided to attack Trenton, New Jersey.

On December 25, 1776, Washington led about 2,400 troops across the Delaware River. On the morning of December 26, 1776, his troops surprised the Hessians at Trenton. The Hessians were German soldiers who worked for the British. Washington took 900 prisoners. Winning this battle raised the spirits of Washington's men. They believed in Washington as a general. The colonists had new hope of winning the war.

THE WINTER AT VALLEY FORGE

Even though Washington's Continental army won the Battle of Trenton, they were not winning the war. In December 1777, Washington and about 10,000 of his soldiers made their winter camp in Valley Forge, Pennsylvania. Valley Forge is about 20 miles (32 kilometers) northwest of Philadelphia.

Washington's soldiers faced the cold, snowy winter without enough supplies or food. By the spring, about one-fourth of the soldiers had died from hunger and from illnesses such as **smallpox**. Washington begged

This engraving shows American troops at Valley Forge. The soldiers were starving and had to wrap their feet in rags to keep them warm.

Baron von Steuben is seen here at Valley Forge. Von Steuben taught Washington's men many skills, including the best method of firing and reloading their weapons.

the Continental Congress to send supplies, and they finally did. Washington also told the congress that the men needed to be better trained.

In February 1778, the congress sent Prussian **volunteer** Baron Friedrich von Steuben to Valley Forge. Washington gave von Steuben the job of training the soldiers. Washington's leadership and von Steuben's expert training paid off when Washington's soldiers fought the British to a draw at the Battle of Monmouth on June 28, 1778.

THE BRITISH SURRENDER AT YORKTOWN

The British controlled the southern part of colonial America in 1780. General Charles Cornwallis was in charge of the British army in this area. Cornwallis set up camp at Yorktown, Virginia, in 1781. Yorktown was near the Chesapeake Bay.

Washington knew he had to act when he heard of Cornwallis's position. He believed he could trap Cornwallis in Yorktown. Washington's plan was made stronger because the French government had agreed to help the Americans.

On September 18, 1781, Washington made a plan with French commanders Comte de Rochambeau and Admiral François Joseph Paul, the Comte de Grasse. They came up with a strategy to attack the British by land and by sea. About 18,000 American and French soldiers and sailors surrounded Yorktown by late September. After a 20-day **siege**, Cornwallis **surrendered**.

Cornwallis's surrender on October 19, 1781, signaled the end of Britain's control of the American colonies. The siege at Yorktown was Washington's greatest victory.

This engraving shows the surrender of the British to George Washington at Yorktown. Cornwallis did not attend the ceremony. He sent his second in command, General Charles O'Hara.

WASHINGTON AND THE U.S. CONSTITUTION

The Americans had won their independence with the surrender at Yorktown. Starting in 1781, Americans followed a set of laws called the Articles of Confederation. The articles gave most of the nation's power to the states. George Washington and other leaders felt that America needed a stronger central government.

In May 1787, representatives from 12 states met at Independence Hall in Philadelphia, Pennsylvania. This convention became known as the Constitutional Convention. Delegates met to create a new constitution instead of trying to fix the Articles of Confederation. Washington was elected the convention's president.

Creating a constitution was not easy. There were many arguments about what to include. Washington helped keep the convention together by helping the members to **compromise**. On September 17, the U.S. Constitution was finished. Washington was the first to sign it. Nine states had to approve the **document** for it to take effect. This happened on June 21, 1788.

This oil painting by Howard Chandler Christy was made in 1940. The subject of the work is the signing of the Constitution of the United States at the Constitutional Convention of 1787.

WASHINGTON BECOMES THE FIRST PRESIDENT OF THE UNITED STATES

With the Constitution approved, George Washington was **unanimously** elected to become the first U.S. president. There were parades and speeches given in his honor. People also wore buttons on their clothes to celebrate this special day. His **inauguration** as president took place at Federal Hall, in New York City, on April 30, 1789.

This illustration shows the inauguration of George Washington as the first president of the United States. The ceremony was done on a balcony above Wall Street. A large crowd cheered after Washington took the oath of office.

George Washington is shown here sitting with his cabinet. From left to right shown here are, President George Washington, Secretary of War General Henry Knox, Secretary of the Treasury Alexander Hamilton, Secretary of State Thomas Jefferson, and Attorney General Edmund Randolph.

As president, Washington chose a **cabinet** of advisers. Each adviser would lead a governmental department. Thomas Jefferson was chosen as secretary of state. He worked to create good relationships with other nations. Henry Knox was in charge of America's defense as secretary of war. Alexander Hamilton became secretary of the treasury, in charge of the nation's money. John Jay was made chief justice, in charge of the nation's courts. Edmund Randolph became the attorney general, or the country's chief lawyer. The creation of a cabinet was one of Washington's greatest presidential contributions.

WASHINGTON RETURNS TO MOUNT VERNON

George Washington served a second term as president from 1793 to 1797. During this term, he worked hard to keep America out of a war between Britain and France. He also put down the Whiskey Rebellion, which was begun by farmers who did not want to pay the tax Washington and Congress placed on whiskey.

This engraving was made to protest a tax created in 1791 by the federal government on whiskey. The tax collector seen here has been tarred and feathered.

This color engraving from 1750 shows Mount Vernon. Washington retired twice to Mount Vernon—once after the war and again after he served as president.

When his second term as president ended in March 1797, George Washington happily returned home to Virginia. Washington's home, Mount Vernon, overlooks the Potomac River. George Washington's half brother had built Mount Vernon. In time Washington bought it. Washington had spent much of his youth on the farm and was pleased to make the property his home.

GEORGE WASHINGTON'S DEATH AND LEGACY

On December 12, 1799, Washington, who was 67 at the time, went out to check on the land of Mount Vernon. The weather was cold and wet. The next day he woke with a sore throat. He became weaker and began to have trouble breathing. He died on December 14, 1799. Washington was buried at Mount Vernon.

George Washington had a major effect on the growth of the United States of America. He was the country's first military leader. He led the Continental army to victory over the British during the American Revolution. He also helped America's leaders solve the problems of forming a democratic government.

Americans honored Washington by naming the nation's capital after him. Washington, D.C., is also home to the Washington Monument. People also go to museums to see paintings and sculptures of him. George Washington has always been and shall always be the father of his country.

GLOSSARY

allies (A-lyz) Countries that support one another.

cabinet (KAB-nit) People who act as advisers to important government officials.

compromise (KOM-pruh-myz) To give up something to reach an agreement.

debts (DETS) Things owed.

document (DOK-yoo-ment) A written or printed statement that gives official information about something.

inauguration (ih-naw-gyuh-RAY-shun) The event of swearing in a government official.

legislature (LEH-jis-lay-chur) A body of people that has the power to make or pass laws.

militia (muh-LIH-shuh) A group of volunteers who are trained and ready to fight in an emergency.

siege (SEEJ) A strong attack.

smallpox (SMOL-poks) A serious and often deadly sickness that causes a rash and leaves marks on the skin.

surrendered (suh-REN-derd) Gave up.

surveying (ser-VAY-ing) Measuring or mapping land.

unanimously (yoo-NA-nih-mus-lee) Having the agreement of all.

volunteer (vah-lun-TEER) Someone who gives his or her time without pay.

INDEX

PRIMARY SOURCE LIST

Page 4: Engraving based on the original portrait of George Washington by John Trumbull (1756-1843). The original painting was started in 1792, finished by 1794, and is housed at the Metropolitan Museum, New York.
Page 9: *Planting Of The Royal Flag On The Ruins Of Fort Du Quesne 1758,* engraving by Louderbach & Hoffman in 1859. Housed at the Art and Picture Collection of the New York Public Library.
Page 11: *Washington Inspecting the Captured Colors after the Battle of Trenton* by Percy Moran (1862-1935). It was created in August of 1914 and is stored at the Prints and Photographs Division, Library of Congress, Washington, D.C.
Page 13: *Baron von Steuben Drilling Washington's Army at Valley Forge* by Edwin Austin Abbey (1852-1911). It is housed at the Pennsylvania State Capitol Building, Harrisburg.
Page 15: *Surrender of Cornwallis: at York-Town VA. Oct. 1781,* published in 1845 by N. Currier, New York.
Page 17: *The Signing of the Constitution of the United States, with George Washington, Benjamin Franklin, and Thomas Jefferson at the Constitutional Convention of 1787,* oil painting from 1940 by Howard Chandler Christy (1873–1952). It hangs in the United States Capitol building.
Page 19: *Washington and His Cabinet,* published in 1876 by Currier & Ives, New York.
Page 20: *An Exciseman,* lithograph by an unknown American artist, in 1790. It is housed at the Philadelphia History Museum at the Atwater Kent.

WEBSITES

Due to the changing nature of Internet links, PowerKids Press has developed an online list of websites related to the subject of this book. This site is updated regularly. Please use this link to access the list: www.powerkidslinks.com/soah/geow